Classic Cat Stevens.

A collection of all the music from four landmark Cat Stevens albums.
Arranged for piano/vocal with guitar frames and full lyrics.

Amsco Publications
New York/London/Sydney

Order No. AM 80029
US International Standard Book Number: 0.8256.1285.3
UK International Standard Book Number: 0.7119.2316.7

Exclusive Distributors:
Music Sales Corporation
257 Park Avenue South, New York, NY 10010 USA
Music Sales Limited
8/9 Frith Street, London W1V 5TZ England
Music Sales Pty. Limited
120 Rothschild Street, Rosebery, Sydney, NSW 2018, Australia

Printed in the United States of America by
Vicks Lithograph and Printing Corporation

Tea For The Tillerman.

Where Do The Children Play?

Words and Music by Cat Stevens

Moderately

Well I think it's fine build - ing jum-bo planes, or tak - ing a ride____ on a

cos - mic train switch on sum-mer from__ a slot ma-chine. Yes

get what you want to if you want,__'cause you can get an - y -thing.__

I know we've come a long___ way,___ we're chang - ing day___ to day,_____

But tell me where do the child - ren play? _____

Well you roll on roads o - ver

fresh green grass, for your lor - ry loads,____ pump-ing

8

Sad Lisa

Words and Music by Cat Stevens

13

Hard-Headed Woman

Words and Music by Cat Stevens

I'm looking for a hard headed woman, One who'll take me for __ my-self, __

And if I find my hard head-ed wom - an __

I won't need _____ no-bod - y else, no, no, no. _____

Copyright © 1970 Salafa Limited.
Administered for the World by Westbury Music Consultants Limited, 56 Wigmore Street, London W1H 9DG.

15

Wild World

Words and Music by Cat Stevens

19

But I Might Die Tonight

Words and Music by Cat Stevens

Slowly

Don't want to work a - way do - in' just what they all say.

Work hard boy, you'll find one day___ you'll have a job like mine.___

'Cause I know for sure no - bod - y should be that poor.

23

Miles From Nowhere

Words and Music by Cat Stevens

Into White

Words and Music by Cat Stevens

A sim - ple gar-den with ac-res of sky, A brown haired dog mouse if___ one dropped by, Yel - low de-lan-ey would sleep well at night._____ With

On The Road To Findout

Words and Music by Cat Stevens

Well I left my hap-py home__ to see what I__ could find out
In the end I'll know__ but on the way__ I won-der
found my-self a-lone__ hop-in' some-one would miss me

I left my folk and friends__ with the aim to clear__ my mind out,
Through des-cend-ing snow__ and thru the frost__ and thun-der,
Think-in' a-bout my home and the last wo-man to kiss me,

Well I hit the row-dy road_____ and
Well I lis-ten to__ the wind come howl __
But some-times you have__ to moan _____ when

33

Father And Son

Words and Music by Cat Stevens

Tea For The Tillerman

Words and Music by Cat Stevens

Bring __ tea for the til - ler - man __ steak for the sun wine __ for the wom - an who made __ the rain come,

Sea - gulls sing __ your hearts a - way __ 'cause while the

Longer Boats

Words and Music by Cat Stevens

44

Teaser And The Firecat.

CAT STEVENS

The Wind

Words and Music by Cat Stevens

Rubylove

Words and Music by Cat Stevens

sky a - bove. Who'll be my light?

You'll be my light, You'll be my

day and night, You'll be mine to - night.

Ah,

Ah. Ah,

54

D. S. al Coda

2.   Ροῦπι Γλυκειά. Ἔλα ξανά
     Ἔλα ξανὰ κοντά μου
     Ἔλα πρωΐ, Μὲ τὴν αὐγὴ
     Ἔσυ σουν σὰν ἥλιου ἀχτίδα
     Ροῦπη μου μικρή

3.   Ruby, my love
     You'll be my love
     You'll be my sky above
     Ruby, my light
     You'll be my light
     You'll be my day and night
     You'll be mine tonight

Changes IV

Words and Music by Cat Stevens

Moderately

Let's all____ start liv - in' liv - in' liv - in' liv - in' for the

one that's going to last. Woah...

If I Laugh

Words and Music by Cat Stevens

If I laugh just a little bit
Maybe I can forget the plans
That I didn't use to get you
At home with me alone

If I laugh just a little bit
Maybe I can recall the way
That I used to be before you
And sleep at night and dream

How Can I Tell You

Words and Music by Cat Stevens

64

thing, hon-ey, and I can't think of right words to say.

say. Oh._____

2. Wherever I am, girl,
   I'm always walking with you,
   I'm always walking with you,
   But I look and you're not there,
   Whoever I'm with I'm always,
   I'm always talking to you,
   I'm always talking to you,
   And I'm sad that you can't hear,
   Sad that you can't hear,
   It always adds up to one thing, honey,
   When I look and you're not there.

3. I need to know you,
   Need to feel my arms around you,
   Feel my arms surround you,
   Like sea around a shore.
   I pray in hope that I might find you,
   In hope that I might find you,
   Because hearts can do no more,
   Can do no more.
   It always ends up to one thing, honey,
   Still I kneel upon the floor.

4. How can I tell you
   That I love you,
   I love you,
   But I can't think of right words to say,
   And I long to tell you
   That I'm always thinking of you,
   I'm always thinking of you,
   But my words just blow away,
   Just blow away.
   It all ends up to one thing, honey,
   And I can't think of right words to say.

Tuesday's Dead

Words and Music by Cat Stevens

Fairly Bright Jamaican (in 2)

If I make a mark in time, I can't say the mark is mine. I'm on - ly the un-

67

Oh preacher won't you paint my dream
won't you show me where you've been,
show me what I haven't seen
to ease my mind
'Cause I will learn to understand
If I have a helping hand
I wouldn't make another demand, all my life
Whoa - where do you go when you don't
want no-one to know
Who told tomorrow - Tuesday's dead

What's my sex, what's my name,
all in all it's all the same
everybody plays a different game - that is all
Now man may live, man may die
searching for the question why,
but if he tries to rule the sky - he must fall
Whoa - where do you go when you don't
want no-one to know
Who told tomorrow - Tuesday's dead
Now every second on the nose
The humdrum of the city grows

Morning Has Broken

Words by Cat Stevens
Musical arrangement by Eleanor Farjeon

1.4. Morn - ing has brok - en like the first morn -
2. Sweet the rain's new fall, sun - lit from heav -

73

Bitterblue

Words and Music by Cat Stevens

Brite Rock

I gave my last chance to you don't hand it back___ to me Bit-ter Blue___
I gave my last hope___ to you don't hand it back___ to me Bit-ter Blue___

No___ Bit-ter Blue
My___ Bit-ter Blue

Moonshadow

Words and Music by Cat Stevens

Peace Train

Words and Music by Cat Stevens

Catch Bull At Four.

CATCH BULL AT FOUR

CAT STEVENS

Sitting

Words and Music by Cat Stevens

94

To Coda

don't need to touch___ your face___ to know, and I don't need
when I'm dead and___ low - ered___ in my grave, there's gon-na be___
keep on push-ing hard, boy. Try___ as you may, you're gon-na wind___

___ to use. my eyes to see.___
___ the on - ly thing that's left of me.

I keep on won-d'ring if I
And___ if I make it to the

sleep too long,___ will I al - ways wake up the same___ (or so)___
wat - er- side,___ will I e - ven find me a boat___ (or so)___

The Boy With The Moon And Star On His Head

Words and Music by Cat Stevens

A gard - ner's daugh - ter stopped me on ___ my way, on the
sil - ver hair ___ flowed ___ in the air, lay - ing

day I was ___ to wed. It is
waves a - cross ___ the sun. Her

you who I wish to share ___ my bod - y with, she
hands were like the white sands, ___ and her eyes had dia monds

us and the un - i -verse a - bove.

(Whistle)

(Sing) The

- round.

There was plen - ty mer - ri - ment, ci - der and wine — a -

- bound. But out of all — that

I re - call, — I re - mem - bered the girl I met,

'cause she had giv-en me some - thing that my heart __ could not for-

- get.

La la __ la la __ la la   la la   la la la __ la la

la la la la __ la la   la la la la   la

in there lay___ the fair - est lit - tle ba - by cry-ing to___ be

fed.   I got down on___ my knees___

___ and kissed___ the moon___ and star   on his

head.

Angelsea

Words and Music by Cat Stevens

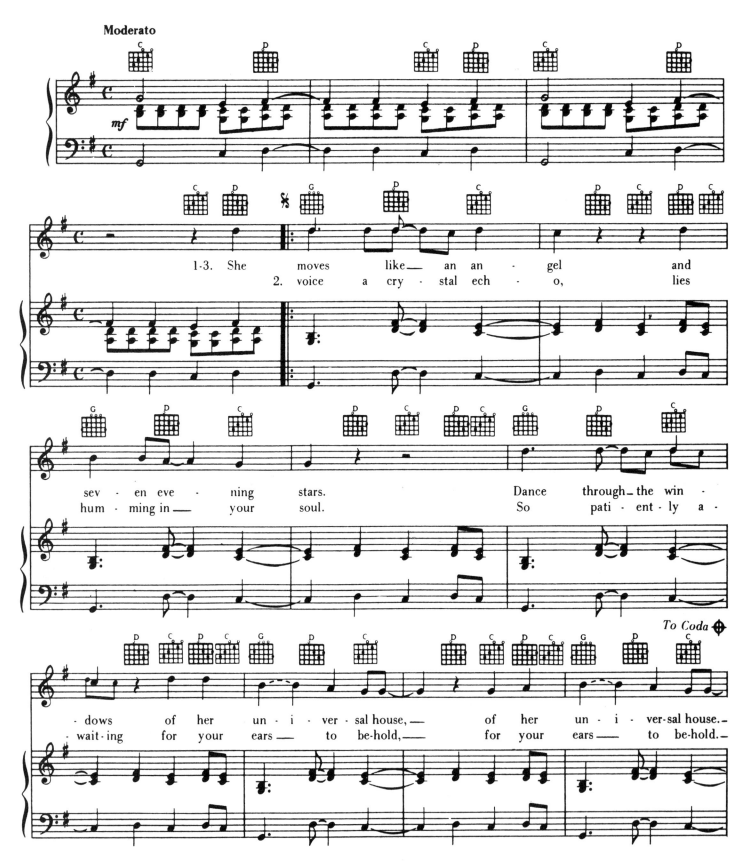

Her   She rip - ples on __ the wa - ter,   leaves

dia - monds on   the shore, __   and   fish from ev - 'ry dis - tance   watch her

113

Silent Sunlight

Words and Music by Cat Stevens

Sil-ent Sun-light wel-come in. There is work I must now be-
song-bird sing a-way. Lend a tune to an-oth-er
hors-es heave a-way. Put your backs to the gol-den

-gin. All my dreams have blown-a-way,— and the
day. Bring your wings and choose-a roof,— sing a
hay. Don't ev-er look be-hind at the work-you've-done,— for your

Can't Keep It In

Words and Music by Cat Stevens

for your love, love ___ heats my blood, blood spins my head and my head ___ falls in love, oh.

No I Can't ___

___ Keep It In, I Can't Keep It In, I've got-ta let it out.

121

122

18th Avenue

Words and Music by Cat Stevens

127

D.S. al Coda

Well I

Coda

time.― Boy, you've made it just in time.

Freezing Steel

Words and Music by Cat Stevens

1 & 4. I've flown the house — of freez - ing, the house of Freez - ing — Steel, —
2. Back on the house — of freez - ing, the house of Freez - ing — Steel, —
3. up on the house — of freez - ing, the house of Freez - ing — Steel, —

and tho' my bod - y's back — I
they tied my bod - y up, — I'm
I made my mind up then — to

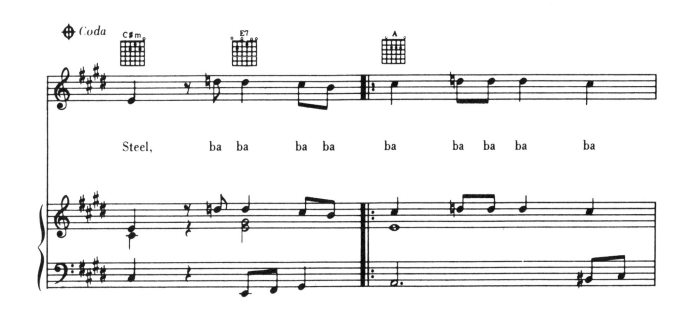

O Caritas

Words and Music by Toumazis, Taylor, and Stevens

143

Ruins

Words and Music by Cat Stevens

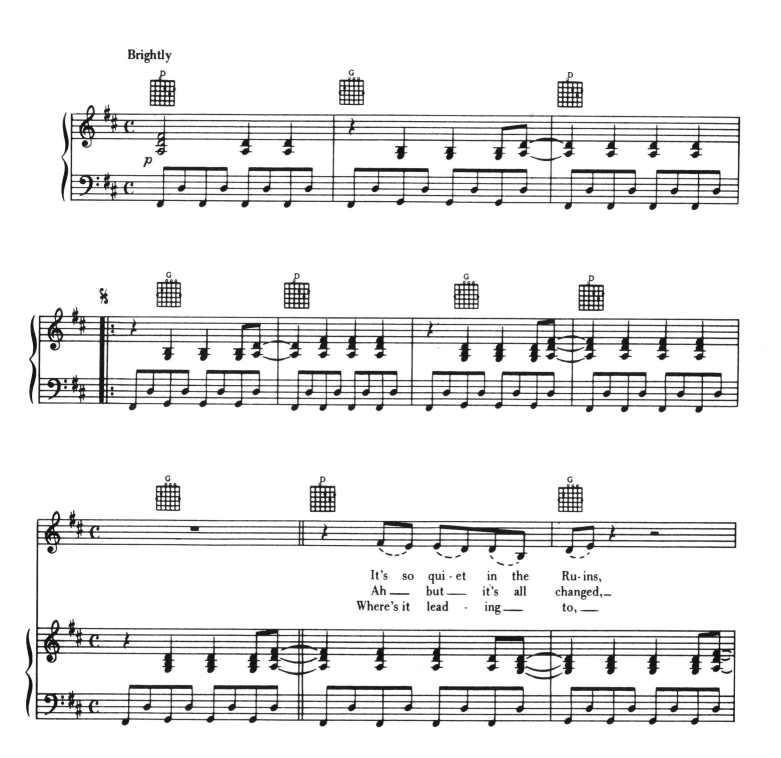

It's so qui - et in the Ru- ins,
Ah — but — it's all changed,—
Where's it lead - ing — to, —

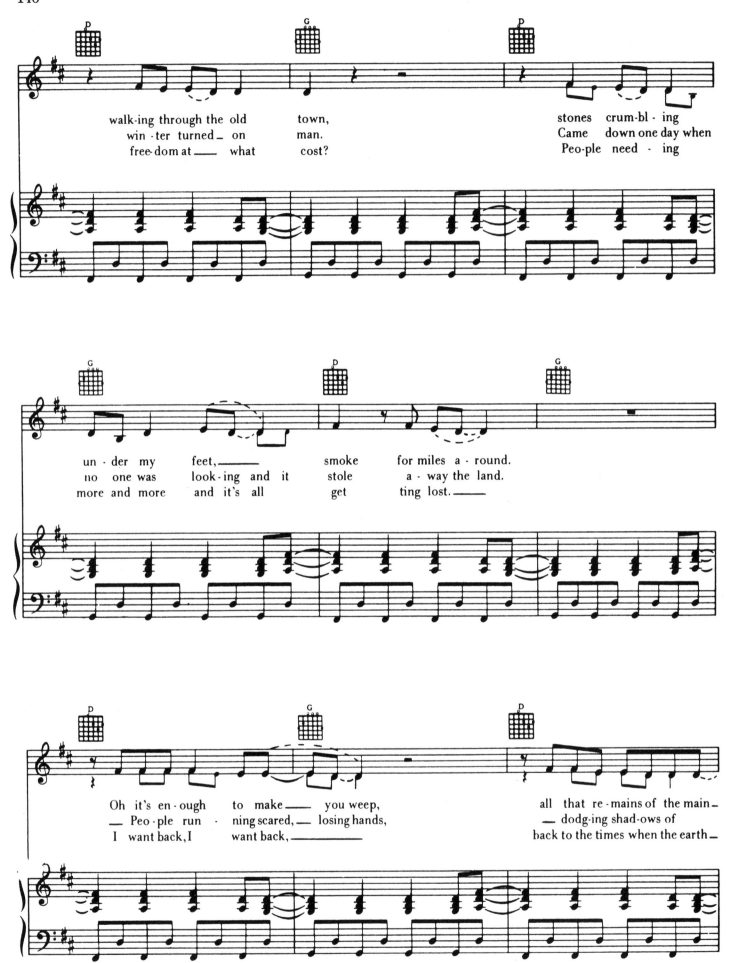

G
D
G
— street. Up in the park on Sun-day,
fall-ing sand. — Build-ings stand-ing like emp-ty shells,
— was green, and there was no high walls and the
D
G
F
dogs chas-ing and the chil-dren played. — Old man with his
and no-bod-y help-ing no one else. — Young child with his
sea was clean. — Don't stop that
mf
C
F
C
A
To Coda
head down, — can't see no-thing more — a-round. (Spoken) No
hands high, — ain't a-ble to see no rea-son why. (Spoken) No
sun to shine. It's not yours or mine. —

So nice to see you com-ing back in this town_ a - gain._

D.S. al Coda

Coda

no._

Sweet Scarlet

Words and Music by Cat Stevens

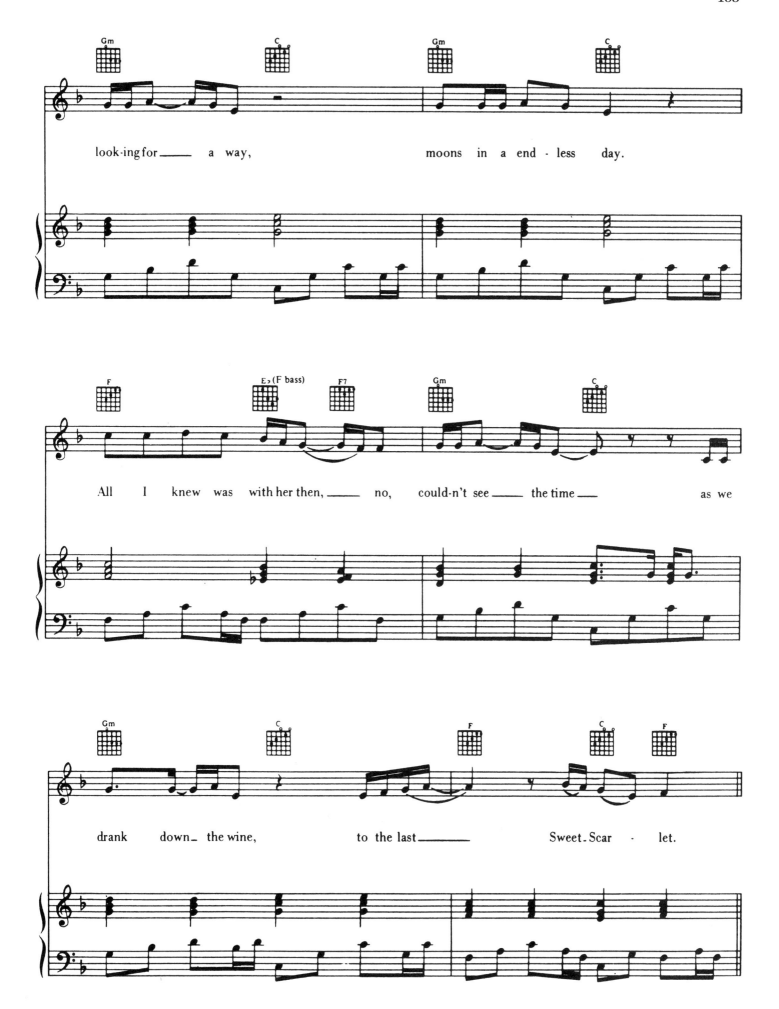

154

157

Buddha And The Chocolate Box.

CAT STEVENS'
BUDDHA AND THE
CHOCOLATE BOX

Music

Words and Music by Cat Stevens

163

Oh Very Young

Words and Music by Cat Stevens

Sun/C79

Words and Music by Cat Stevens

back in suite seven-ty nine

I'll nev-er, nev-er for-get

I'll nev-er for-get that time

back on the road a-gain

Oh I'm trav-'ling that line

I was a pop star then

I'm

still hav-ing a good time

Repeat ad lib. and fade

Ghost Town

Words and Music by Cat Stevens

Come on____ let's go__ down ev - 'ry-bod -y's wai -ting for us

down at the ghost town____

Ready

Words and Music by Cat Stevens

183

King Of Trees

Words and Music by Cat Stevens

He was the king of the trees keep-er of __ the leaves

a deep green god of young love stained memory __

We used to meet by __ him

far from the hustling town I loved you __ now they've come to cut you down __ down

187

A Bad Penny

Words and Music by Cat Stevens

Jesus

Words and Music by Cat Stevens

Home In The Sky

Words and Music by Cat Stevens

198